COSMIC!

DONCASTER

Edited by Dave Thomas

First published in Great Britain in 1998 by
POETRY NOW YOUNG WRITERS
1-2 Wainman Road, Woodston,
Peterborough, PE2 7BU
Telephone (01733) 230748

HB ISBN 0 75430 217 2
SB ISBN 0 75430 218 0

FOREWORD

With over 63,000 entries for this year's Cosmic competition, it has proved to be our most demanding editing year to date.

We were, however, helped immensely by the fantastic standard of entries we received, and, on behalf of the Young Writers team, thank you.

The Cosmic series is a tremendous reflection on the writing abilities of 8-11 year old children, and the teachers who have encouraged them must take a great deal of credit.

We hope that you enjoy reading *Cosmic Doncaster* and that you are impressed with the variety of poems and style with which they are written, giving an insight into the minds of young children and what they think about the world today.

CONTENTS

Dean Bower	64
Daniel Hewitt	65
Daniel Parkin	65
Libby Velta Antons-Jones	66
Paul Dyer	66
Liam Stephenson	67
Peter Meakin	67
Mark Allinson	68
Bree Fox	68
Rebecca Jane England	69
Gemma Mulholland	69
Alan Biddleston	70
Ashley Le Gat	70

Shaw Wood Junior School

Amy Neidhardt	71
Jessica Smith	71
Jodie Polson	71
Rachel Doran	72
Kirsty Tucker	72
Lee Needham	73
Jade Harper	73
Matthew Varley	74
Ross Wilson	74
Kerrie Curry	75
Carla Louise Drane	75
Michael Varley	76
Amanda Standring	76
Shorrel Benjamin	77
Nadine Benjamin	77
Melissa Steptoe	78

Walkeringham Primary School

Laura Howard	78
Jonathan Scott	79
Oliver White	79
Nico Vaccari	79
Louise Barlow	80

Heidi Clinch	80
Brett Myers	81
Marc Priest	81
Kathryn Price	82
Matthew Howard	82
Sam Bramham	83
Wayne Cockin	83
Daniel Staples	84
Sam Lowther	84
Robert Baxter	85
James Hardy	85

Willow Primary School

Hannah Miller	86
Joanna Henshaw	87
Elliot Gale	88
Samantha Whiteley	88
Alastair Brown	88
Richard Hinchliffe	89
Henry Beevor	89
Vicki Lacey	90
Michael Frosdick	90
Paul Richardson	91
Rebecca A Sykes	91
Thomas White	92
Nyssa Blake	92
Matthew Payne	93
Scott Chattin	93
Rachel Haigh	94
Oliver Churchill	94
Claire Wragg	95
Michael Peterson	95
Christopher Buckley	96
Laura Wilbourn	96
Hannah Shekle	97
Sharlene Duhre	97
Kim Norman	98
William Coleman	98

Tiffany Hankinson	99
Jessica Barras	99
Kathryn McColl	100
Emma Warren	100
Melissa Oxley	101
Samantha Crowther	101
Dominic Caunt	102
Thomas Falcon	102
Antony Lunn	103
Amadeus Usher	103
Samantha Shaw	104
Racheal Purchase	104
Sophia Chambers	105
Victoria Ford	105
Emily Wykes	106
Kathryn Foster	106
Carl Tipper	107
Nadia Akhtar	107
Sara Horscroft	108
Francesca Salt	108
Nicky Hetherington	109
Thomas Goodman	109
Jade McDermott	110
Alice Tucker	110
Bethany Smith	111

THE POEMS

PRINCESS DIANA
(To Nanna and Grandad)

It was a night, one lonely night
that no one would forget,
where the Princess of all our hearts
was killed and left to rest.
She'd been running away all her life
and now she could finally stop,
while her beautiful eyes and gleaming smile
will never be forgot.
She was so kind to others
no matter how good or bad,
and when we thing of her it makes us feel so sad.
She was the Queen of all our hearts
and healed us with our touch,
and as she gave us hope and love
it made us feel so good.
For she was like a mother
to every boy and girl,
by caring and protecting us
all around the world.
But now she's gone for ever
and that makes us feel so mad,
for we all loved her dearly
and she was the best the nation's had.

Laura Mitchell (12)
Campsmount School

SIMILES 12

As thin as a piece of string,
as thick as a bus.
As big as a block of flats,
as little as a poppy seed.
As cold as a bath of ice cubes,
as hot as the sun.
As blunt as a needle,
as sharp as a knife.
As nasty as a purple monster,
as kind as a kitten.
As bright as the luminous moon,
as dull as a foggy day.
As sad as a tiger with no stripes,
as light as the sun.
As dark as a cave,
as rough as a tree.
As smooth as a grape,
as straight as a shelf.
As wiggly as a worm,
as messy as a dump.
As tidy as an office.

Jennifer Jeffrey (8)
Hawthorn Primary School

THE MURDERER'S CRIMES

I found shadowy tracks at night.
I saw a tired horseman get stabbed.
Bridges were broken.
The words of prayers had been stolen.
Voices told lies, not promises.

Kaine Ridge (9)
Hawthorn Primary School

A HAMSTER

There was once,
A hamster called
Hammy.
He scampered around
His little cage.
He slept in the day,
And he talked at night.
When he came to his
Food and said 'Yummy,
Yum, yum!'
He said to his water,
'Woo I need a wash,'
So he went up to
His water and had a wash,
He played with his ball,
On top of his cage.
He said, 'That's it,
That's my day!'

Rachel Walton (10)
Hawthorn Primary School

THE UNHAPPINESS OF MAN

I glimpsed a crying man
with pained stilted shoulders.
He was soaked in salt
Death wasting his teeth.
He had endured many hurt and torn years.

Sarah Edgecombe (9)
Hawthorn Primary School

BASKETBALL

My basketball coach is tall and slim,
My basketball coach is fast and fun,
My basketball coach is great and exciting,
My basketball coach gets sweaty and hot,
My basketball coach is fast and noisy,
My basketball coach is great and skilful.

Kelly Williams (11)
Hawthorn Primary School

SIMILES 9

As big as a giant, as small as a fairy.
As cute as a mouse, as ugly as a troll.
As straight as a pencil, as bent as a bridge.
As smooth as fur, as rough as a rock.
As full as a can, as empty as a dustbin.
As helpful as a grandma, as unhelpful as a weed.

Laura Edmunds (8)
Hawthorn Primary School

THE WORLD

The running stream dripping with salt,
Wept, soaking its pained shoulders.
Torn ploughed teeth, wasting away
Whispered death with crying eyes,
To the helpless breeze.

Sean Chapman (9)
Hawthorn Primary School

SNOWFALL

White, fresh, icy snow,
It's so cold that marbled tears flow.
The tired rivers, so deep and dark
are now frozen over, crystal clear with not a mark.
All the treetops, all the rocks, plus every single garden
are all covered with a soft, white, velvet carpet.

Leanne Fox (10)
Hawthorn Primary School

THE SHADOWS

The shadows on the door
on a silent night,
Would give me thoughts
of a horrible fright,
My bones would shiver
I would think of blood.

Emma Teale (10)
Hawthorn Primary School

EARTH

Smooth precious shells lie on a soft grey beach,
Cold desolate rivers run to the stormy sea.
The laughter and fire of lost flowers whose
rich soul is now thorny and ragged.
People wrestle with nature on this dark, dark, cold night.
The branch of the tree is falling.

John Cowley (10)
Hawthorn Primary School

SIMILES 9

As narrow as a lamppost, as wide as a bus.
As cold as the South Pole, as hot as Africa.
As hard as metal, as soft as fur.
As dark as night, as bright as the sun.
As small as a crumb, as big as a tower.
As colourful as a rainbow, as dull as fog.
As strong as the sea, as weak as a rubber.

Louise Cairns (9)
Hawthorn Primary School

WAR!

The broken tortured horseman,
With cruel swollen promises.
Stolen prayers flood mothers' minds,
Shadows on an ancestral wall,
Voices sound from nowhere,
Bridges knocked down by murderous bombs,
Tanks full of promises set off to war!

Lisa Buckley (9)
Hawthorn Primary School

THE CASTLE OF WISDOM

The fate of a miserable tongue,
with robbed, hopeless lies.
The now silent, crooked castle of wisdom.
The stilled sound of the hounds stalking tracks,
The guards lurch upon the kings
velvet guns with five dangerous jewels.

Samantha Taylor (9)
Hawthorn Primary School

THE SPARROWHAWK AND FOOD

Here comes the sparrowhawk,
Gliding through the air
Looking for something he can rip.
His claws, so sharp, grasp hold of his victims
Suddenly he lands with a swoop.
Here he searches.
He sees a vole.
The vole scuttles along the grass.
He spots the sparrowhawk and dashes for his life
The sparrowhawk chasing him as fast as he can.
Eventually when all is victorious, the sparrowhawk
Captures the poor little vole.
Next he spies a kestrel flying along.
But he doesn't eat it.
I wonder why?
Because he has had enough food for one day.

Bindi Eyre (10)
Hawthorn Primary School

DESTRUCTION

The smooth cold stone lay buried in the sand,
deserted for years and years in some faraway land.

The taut ragged cliffs have lost their soul and laughter
dripping with grief tortured by thoughtless actions.

The forests calm and still, waiting to be torn apart
gloomy with the pain to come.

Kerrie Luke (11)
Hawthorn Primary School

ONE DAY I MET AN ALIEN

One day I saw an alien
I said 'You look scary.'
'I'm not, I'm always weary.'
He shook hands, they were hairy.

One day I saw an alien
I said to him 'You're small,'
'No I'm not, I'm tall
You're heading for a fall!'

One day I met an alien
I said 'You look like a rock.'
'Come here and I'll give you a right knock.'
Bash, bang, sock!

One day I met an alien
I walked away, it's not the right day!

Carl Tunmore (9)
Hawthorn Primary School

THE LAUGHING EYE

The rich fire of the soul
The laughter of my sister's eye
The soft cold sand
The ancient smooth stones
The grief of the lost rivers
The hunger of my brother's wisdom
The shells formed through the years
The ragged soldiers in the halls.

Jonathan Hancock (10)
Hawthorn Primary School

COOKIE CHOMPER THE CHIPMUNK

Cookie chomper,
Is a chipmunk,
For short we call him Chip
He adores to give,
You a kiss on the lips
And sometimes likes to eat chips.
You find them easily
For you'll find him
Up a tree gathering coconuts.
At night he snores
And tries to roar
And twists and turns and rolls.
So in the end,
He's had enough.
So he sleeps on the floor and snores.

Kayleigh Davis (9)
Hawthorn Primary School

EARTH

The smooth soft shells and the ragged
ancient rivers showed the years of rich
flowers and the strength of cold stones.
In the sandy cliffs they were thorns and
they pricked me. It hurt my soul.
The sky was blue and the rivers flowed all around.
Tears dripped when the flowers died.
The rivers flooded and the land dissolved.

Carl Hinsley (11)
Hawthorn Primary School

SIMILES 3

As weak as a kitten, as strong as a weight-lifter,
As good as a gold star, as naughty as a puppy dog,
As rough as a raptor, as smooth as skin,
As soft as a sponge, as hard as a brick wall,
As straight as a pen, as bent as a banana,
As asleep as you can be, as awake as a bumble-bee,
As bored as a baby, as interesting as the world can be,
As kind as a kitty, as cruel as a cheetah,
As clever as a class, as dumb as a duck,
As thick as a pig, as thin as a wasp,
As bright as the sun, as dull as a door,
As old as the universe, as young as a newborn baby,
As empty as a bowl can be, as full as a dustbin.

Nathan Jones (7)
Hawthorn Primary School

THE ROBBER AND MURDER

The necklace was robbed.
Everyone telling lies.
The crooked key.
The grim guard.
The sadness and silence were hopeless.
No one had golden wisdom.
Overhead their was a gunshot.
Then a deserted silence.

Jessica Duncan (10)
Hawthorn Primary School

GRUB THE ALIEN

He hovered down in a flash of light
The boogie-eyed alien.
He clambered out on a starlit night
Where he jogged across the road.
There he saw a local pub,
Sneakily he sloped in,
Asking for their very best grub,
Then he began to tuck in.
When he was lull and terribly drunk,
He staggered across the highway
And got back into the hidden light,
And broke the space limit of 30 zorbways.

Rhiannon Smith (10)
Hawthorn Primary School

LADYBIRD

I found a ladybird
One summer's day,
And at first I told him
To go away.
He said to me,
'You ugly thing,
It's a free country,
I can do
Anything!'

Jessica Jeffrey (10)
Hawthorn Primary School

SIMILES (6)

As spiky as a thorny tree, as smooth as silk,
As dirty as a pig, as clean as a freshly bathed child,
As rough as a rock, as smooth as fur,
As quiet as a mouse, as loud as a barking dog,
As full as a bin, as empty as a clean sheet of paper,
As bright as the sun, as dull as fog,
As soft as a rubber toy, as hard as metal,
As straight as a pencil, as bent as a hump-backed bridge,
As sad as a crying baby, as happy as a bird,
As cruel as a bat, as kind as a teacher,
As old as a cottage, as new as a newborn baby.

Rebecca Parkin (8)
Hawthorn Primary School

SIMILE 5

As empty as a pea pod, as full as a shopping trolley,
As soft as a butterfly, as hard as a concrete slab,
As good-mannered as an insect, as bad-mannered as a bully,
As living as you, as dead as a dinosaur,
As tall as the universe, as small as a germ,
As straight as a ruler, as bent as a joint,
As rough as a porcupine, as smooth as cats,
As stiff as a piece of metal, as flexible as your spine,
As foggy as Christmas Day, as clear as a window.

John McKeon (9)
Hawthorn Primary School

SIMILES 14

As rough as a rock, as smooth as fur.
As straight as a door, as bent as a camel's hump.
As bright as the north star, as dull as rain.
As tall as a giant, as small as a crumb.
As kind as Mum, as cruel as a hunter.
As helpful as a servant, as unhelpful as an ant.
As soft as silk, as hard as a hammer.
As smooth as an apple, as rough as sandpaper.
As fast as a car, as slow as a snail.
As interesting as a historical book, as boring as a green welly.
As thick as a wall, as thin as paper.

Melissa Crowther (8)
Hawthorn Primary School

SIMILES 8

As black as a crow, as white as paper.
As spiky as pins, as smooth as hair.
As bright as the sky, as dull as night.
As soft as an armchair, as hard as a brick.
As cheerful as a bird, as sad as death.
As helpful as a servant, as unhelpful as war.
As dusty as chalk, as clean as a car.
As light as the sun, as dark as tarmac.
As tall as a five-storey building, as small as a seed.

David Livsey (9)
Hawthorn Primary School

BASKETBALL

Basketball is fantastic fun
Played in a gym or out in the sun.
Shoot for a basket, dunk it in one
Two more points, we've nearly won.
Off the backboard or off the rim,
The hooter sounds when the ball drops in.
No double dribble or travelling too.
No body contact or it's a foul against you.
Lightning passes really count,
Feeling tired, let's take time out.

Siobhan Fear (10)
Hawthorn Primary School

SIMILES 7

As thin as a worm - as thick as a wall,
As small as a mouse - as big as a bear,
As straight as a pencil - as bent as a bridge,
As spiky as a hedgehog - as smooth as fur,
As bright as the sun - as dull as mist,
As bored as a child - as unhelpful as a brother,
As clever as a person - as dumb as a cat,
As fast as a hare - as slow as a tortoise,
As kind as a mum - as cruel as a child.

Samantha Livsey (8)
Hawthorn Primary School

SIMILES 13

As clever as a baby, as dumb as a clown.
As cold as water, as hot as the sun.
As thick as an encyclopaedia, as thin as a stick.
As rough as a path, as smooth as a window.
As black as a pen, as white as paper.
As hard as a door, as soft as fur.
As spiky as a hedgehog, as smooth as hair.
As straight as a book, as bent as a bridge.
As nice as an apple, as horrible as a carrot.
As kind as a teacher, as cruel as a witch.

Kate Touhig (8)
Hawthorn Primary School

EARTH

The wasting mourning streams
once loved, now pained.
The hurting with lined
shoulders.
Death just moments away,
fields crying and ragged.
The Earth weeps silently.
Years disappear into bleached, scorched trees.

Desolation!

Jamie Ruddock (10)
Hawthorn Primary School

THE SNAKE AND THE FLEA

There once was a snake who had no friends,
until he came to a lake.
He was washing himself when he heard a voice,
which was smaller than you can make.
It was a flea, which said with glee.
'Oh please don't wash me off,
your skin is so rough and slimy.'
The snake replied, 'You think mine is rough,
well, that's just tough.'
'Oh blimey!'

Peter Long (11)
Hawthorn Primary School

SIMILES 10

As big as a fair, as small as an ant.
As fast as a car, as slow as a snail.
As wobbly as jelly, as still as a statue.
As warm as a fire, as cold as ice.
As straight as an arrow, as bent as a corner.
As prickly as a hedgehog, as smooth as silk.
As soft as snow, as hard as a rock.
As bright as yellow, as dull as fog.
As boring as pencils, as interesting as science.
As clever as God, as dumb as a clown.

Darrell Creed (9)
Hawthorn Primary School

ARMISTICE DAY

Bright red poppies standing
in a field. All the soldiers
winning a shield.

Soldiers standing with all
their might.
Ready to fight on a
dark winter's night.

Women crying whilst
their husbands are dying.

Women crying loudly.

Funerals are sad,
The war has been bad.

Soldiers hide as the bombs
fly inside.

Children playing in
the park, whilst their dad
dies in
the dark.

Bethany Holmes (10)
Ivanhoe JI School

SOLDIERS AT WAR

Bang! Hear the guns shooting.
Black cannonballs *whooshing* through the twilight night.
Running to the razor sharp barbed wire.
Hearing your mates calling for your help.

Gary Connelly (11)
Ivanhoe JI School

AUTUMN COLOURS

Autumn colours in the air,
On the trees and everywhere.
Brown, orange, red and green,
Any colour you could dream.
There are noises here and there,
Autumn trees are almost bare.

Autumn leaves turning brown,
See the people looking round,
Squirrels go and get their stock,
Nuts and berries in their pack.
Children playing in the leaves,
Someone's thrown them in the breeze.

Conkers, conkers everywhere!
Conkers, conkers fill the air,
Turn from green,
Then to brown.
Children start and play all day,
Then the little children say:-
'Conkers, conkers everywhere,
Conkers, conkers fill the air.'

Joanne Laird (11)
Ivanhoe JI School

ARMISTICE DAY

Cannonball, big, black and loud,
See the clouds going nearer to the ground.
Women cry as their husbands die,
See the blood coming from their eyes.
See the ditch, brown, deep and muddy,
Filled with water, nearly flooding.

Tony Clyde (11)
Ivanhoe JI School

POPPY APPEAL

Mould on bread
Next to a bleeding head.
Cold and runny
Not very funny.
All you can see in
Front of the sun
Bombs and explosions
And shooting guns,
People have bled
'Quick, fetch the thread!'
People running, soldiers gunning
The war is
Far from done.
People running in the night.
See them fastened to a barbed wire fence.
This is why the Poppy Appeal is
Celebrated every year.

Aaron Bowen (11)
Ivanhoe JI School

ARMISTICE DAY

See the poppies standing in the field
Watching the soldiers being attended and healed.

Watch the soldiers standing in the cold,
Listening to the cannonballs explode.

Listen to the soldiers walking in the night
They have to get up and prepare to fight.

Katie Grainger (10)
Ivanhoe JI School

AUTUMN IS COMING

The season's changing, autumn is here,
The conkers are falling from the trees.
All of the leaves are on the ground,
Be careful, you might slip,
It's getting cold, it is night.

Conkers falling to the ground,
All the leaves swirling round.
All the children come to play,
The woodland animals run away.

Spiky conkers in the tree,
Then the squirrel finds them,
And throws them at me!
All the leaves are swirling and twirling
In the breeze
Then one lands on me!

Thomas Parkes (10)
Ivanhoe JI School

SUNDAY FOOTBALL

As I awoke on Sunday morn,
The first thing I did was check the lawn.
Was this the day that I would score,
Or just another goalless draw?
The manager told us not to worry,
After all, it's not for money.
The time had come for us to play,
But not for me I'm sad to say.

Nicky Bircumshaw (10)
Ivanhoe JI School

AUTUMN

Autumn leaves turn golden brown.
See them falling to the ground.
Acorns falling through the air,
While squirrels are climbing everywhere,
Hiding nuts in the ground,
When he can't find them, he has a frown.

Conkers falling through the trees,
They are falling by our knees.
Children picking them off the ground,
See leaves swirling round.

Autumn comes, the conkers are brown.
See them falling to the ground.
The leaves are rustling round and round.
They make a crunching, scuffling sound.

Natasha Berry (11)
Ivanhoe JI School

ARMISTICE DAY

Soldiers on the ground, faces in the mud.
When it's over, survivors get up.
And lift their heads.
See the people lying dead.
And also see the poppies red.
And that is why to this day,
We celebrate in this way,
To remember the dead
With a poppy red.

Dane Irish (10)
Ivanhoe JI School

ARMISTICE DAY

Soldiers watching
               poppies grow red
      Amongst their friends
Who will soon
      be dead.
          Wishing they were
asleep in bed.
          While they sit there eating
all their bread.
              Seeing all their
friends who are already dead.
          Listening to the guns load
and explode.
          Then suddenly you're
dead!

Jay Shephard (11)
Ivanhoe JI School

AUTUMN IS COMING

Autumn is coming nearer every day,
Children go to the lane to play.

With the wind and rain,
Autumn has come again.

Squirrels running up and down the trees,
The leaves are blowing in the breeze.

A fox is looking for something to eat,
He might like a bit of meat.

Fiona Garth (10)
Ivanhoe JI School

ARMISTICE DAY

Poppies red, lots of them dead,
Soldiers eating mouldy bread,
Soldiers wishing they were in their bed.

Cannonballs big, black, heavy and loud,
See the clouds go nearer to the ground.

Women cry as their husbands die,
Why was it done?

Lots of barbed wire,
While buildings are on fire.

People are led,
To their wet bed.

Dale Scott (11)
Ivanhoe JI School

POPPY APPEAL

Mould on bread, next to a bleeding head,
Cold and runny, not very funny,
All you can see in front of the sun,
Bombs and explosions, shooting guns,
People have bled. Quick! Fetch the thread!
People running, soldiers gunning,
The war is far from done.
People running through the night.
See them fastened to the barbed wire fence.
This is why the Poppy Appeal is celebrated every year.

Rebecca Frost (10)
Ivanhoe JI School

AUTUMN

Autumn leaves turn brown,
See the people with a frown.
Squirrels collect their winter stack,
Putting them in a tree's crack.

> Conkers are ripe, ready to play,
> Children, to collect them, wait all day.
> Children throw things up in the trees,
> To get the conkers for you and me.

See the people with a frown,
As they look all around.
Leaves and conkers all go brown,
As they fall to the ground.

Matthew Evans (11)
Ivanhoe JI School

ARMISTICE DAY

People screaming and shouting,
Fields are red, people are dead,
People crying,
Everyone dying,
Bombs exploding,
Guns reloading,
Young men moaning,
Old men groaning
No more . . .
War's because people are poor,
We say goodbye to people who die.

Kyle Roberts (11)
Ivanhoe JI School

ARMISTICE DAY

People screaming, shouting
Fields are red
People are dead
People crying.

Everyone dying
Bombs exploding
Guns loading.

Young men groaning
Old men moaning
We say goodbye.

To all the people who die.

Kerry Bolland (10)
Ivanhoe JI School

THE WAR'S LIGHT

The war light goes dark,
The men stop, ready for battle,
Big shells waiting for firing,
The war light goes darker,
Men marching,
Others firing,
Women crying for their husbands dying,
Big banging cannonballs,
Firing across the bloody fields,
The light goes bright,
Another new day has come.

Michael Phillips (10)
Ivanhoe JI School

ARMISTICE DAY

Soldiers go, looking bold,
It does not matter how old.
They were not carrying much gold.
They wondered, 'Will I survive in the cold?'
Bang!
Some of the soldiers are dead,
See the blood, bright and red.
White and pale look their head,
Wives alone, asleep in bed,
Wondering, 'Is my husband dead?'

Why oh why did they have to die?
People cry as they look at the sky.

Leigha Charity (11)
Ivanhoe JI School

AUTUMN

The leaves are falling off the trees,
There is a nasty breeze,
I get shivers in my knees.

All the leaves are brown,
They keep falling to the ground,
I hear a crackling sound.

All the potatoes are in a sack,
All the onions are on a rack,
All the carrots are in a pack,
All ready to go on a tractor's back.

Claire Green (11)
Ivanhoe JI School

RED POPPIES

See the red poppy lying dead,
See all the people wearing them,
Look at the people who were injured,
Just take two minutes to remember them.

See the poppies red, see the people shooting red,
See the people's bleeding head.
People crying, people sighing,
See the people's friend crying for them.

See the black cannon shooting the dark night
Wishing they were sleeping in bed,
Instead of fighting for their breath.

Daniel Hornung (10)
Ivanhoe JI School

AUTUMN

Summer is over, winter is near,
Frost is on its way,
Cold in the morning, cold at night,
Every single day.

Trees bending down,
Conkers falling all around,
The trees are brown,
All around.
Leaves are changing colour,
As the wind blows
The trees more strongly.

Antony Rufus (11)
Ivanhoe JI School

SOLDIERS AT WAR

See the poppies standing
In the field,
Watching the soldiers being
attended and healed.
Watch the soldiers standing
in the cold.
Listen to the cannon
balls heavily explode.
Listen to the soldiers walking
In the night.
They have to get up
and prepare to fight.

Mathew Belfield (11)
Ivanhoe JI School

AUTUMN

As I lock my door with a key.
I always see the great oak tree.
Each autumn, leaves come off the tree.

    Fall to the ground.
    Swirl all around.

Wind strips the leaves
From the old oak tree
We go down on our bare knees.

    Picking up the rotten leaves,
    In the cold we start to freeze.

Judy Jones (11)
Ivanhoe JI School

IN A TRENCH

In the trenches with the mud,
Stained clothes with the blood,
Also with the rotting wood,
Trying to buy more ammunition.
I wish they could.
In this big war,
With all the gore,
I think it's beginning to pour.
The rats are beginning to gnaw,
More and more on the people at war.
They are beginning to shoot.
The air is beginning to pollute.

Gary McCabe (10)
Ivanhoe JI School

SNAKE

Waiting
    for
      prey
        He
      slithers
          on
        the
      grass
    Hiding
    and
  hungry
    Waiting
      and
      killing!

Cain Ahmed (8)
King Edward Primary School

MY SPOOKY POEM

I can hear heavy rain, tapping on the window,
I can hear thunder, crashing deafeningly,
I can see shadows, creeping alarmingly,
I can see huge puddles, growing very quickly,
Then suddenly comes a ghost . . .

It creeps up to me and I have to sneeze,
What am I going to do now?
My heart starts beating faster and faster,
Until it feels like it's pounding out of my body!

I can feel the spirits coming over me,
I can feel braveness a bit, I look scared
But I feel very confident,
I can imagine ghosts spookily crossing this room,
I can imagine black spiders quietly making
Their webs in the corner of the room.

I start to panic and wonder which way
To go, which way? I do not know.
I need to shout for help but no sounds come out
I run with fear, the ghosts are laughing in my head,
I don't know what's going to happen,
But soon enough I'm going to leave here.

All at once, everything is still!
All at once, everything is quiet!
Where are the ghosts now?
Gone away - like the storm

Helen Greenley (10)
King Edward Primary School

THE THUNDERSTORM - MY SPOOKY POEM

It was the middle of the night.
It was dark and I shivered with fright.
A storm had brewed up, and the wind made
                              the window-sills rattle,
Which let in a draught and made me feel rather cold.

There was a sudden flash of lightning
Which made my room aglow with dancing shadows.
The wind sounded like the groaning of a ghost,
Which made me feel I wasn't alone!

The thunder sounded like the wailing of a monster.
There was a sudden crash! Which shocked me the most.
I went downstairs to investigate this racket.
My shadows crept downstairs with me as if they,
                              too, were curious.

I walked through the hall as the storm rolled on,
Got to the kitchen and slightly opened the door,
Then I saw a shadow which nearly made me scream,
I turned on the light and then I caught sight of my
                              father raiding the fridge.

He looked as scared as me so as quiet as could be,
I crept back upstairs, which now looked rather normal.
I climbed into bed, with the thought in my head that
                              thunderstorms aren't spooky at all.

James Wilson (9)
King Edward Primary School

THE POPPY FIELD

Poppies are bright red
Poppies grow so quickly
Poppies smell like grass.

Louise Hanson (9)
King Edward Primary School

SKY

The blue sky up high
The sky is like a blue sheet
The sky is soft blue.

Richard Tyas (9)
King Edward Primary School

THE POPPIES

Poppies are pretty
The poppies are elegant
They are delicate.

Harriet Payne (9)
King Edward Primary School

DAFFODILS

Daffodils are sweet
They are bright like the sunshine
Blowing in the breeze.

Alishia Bisby (7)
King Edward Primary School

SPRING

In spring flowers grow,
In the spring rabbits are born.
So are baby lambs.

Robert Clarke (8)
King Edward Primary School

DAFFODILS

Daffodils are nice.
They are bright and colourful.
They make me happy.

Stacey Jay Bagnall (8)
King Edward Primary School

THE SPRING

I like white snowdrops.
Animals are born in spring.
Blossom comes in spring.

Hayley Smith (9)
King Edward Primary School

THE POPPIES

The sun shines all day
The poppies dance in the wind
The birds are singing.

Nigel Hoyle, Luke Busby (8)
*   & Jamie Barry (9)*
King Edward Primary School

SUMMER

Hot sun
Have cold drinks
Playing on the sand
Cool!

Rebecca Blinkhorn (7)
King Edward Primary School

RUNNING

Good exercise
Sweaty and tired
I enjoy racing around
Sports.

Leanne Hardy (8)
King Edward Primary School

HORSES

Beautiful eyes
Extend their trot
Galloping over the fields
Ride.

Lorna Wood (8)
King Edward Primary School

FLOWERS

Bright colours
Dancing wild heads
Making the garden beautiful
In summer.

Hannah Thomas (8)
King Edward Primary School

SWIMMING

Great sport,
Very big splash,
Feeling soggy and wet,
Breast stroke.

Jason Hardy (8)
King Edward Primary School

HORSES

Tall, beautiful
Trot all day
Stroking their lovely manes
Gallop.

Sammie Prior (8)
King Edward Primary School

HOLIDAY

Sea, sun
Travelling on aeroplanes
I've been to Majorca
Cool!

Michael Johnson (8)
King Edward Primary School

CARS

Engines, noisy.
Racing around the track.
My favourite one winning.
F-a- a-a-a-st!

Aaron Jones (8)
King Edward Primary School

HORSES

Brown, white
Walking, trotting, galloping.
They are so beautiful,
Riding.

Kirsty Baxter (7)
King Edward Primary School

WHAT IS YELLOW?

Daffodils grow
yellow and bright.
Like saffron sizzling in a pan.
I like yellow.
It's the colour of the sun.

Sarah Knowles (9)
King Edward Primary School

DINOSAURS

Huge, massive
Flesh-eating lizards
Looking fierce and scary.
Monsters!

John Guest (9)
King Edward Primary School

FAMILY

Mum, Dad
Fighting, always arguing
I love them both
Together.

Aimee Brown (8)
King Edward Primary School

SPOOKY! MY STORM POEM

The puddles are gigantic and they're growing drastically!
But . . . *Aaahhh!* There is a ghost, hovering.
But I'm not scared . . . *Am I?*
The attic door is creaking,
and the attic ghost is sneaking!
But I'm not scared . . . *Am I?*
The rain is pouring,
and this is boring!
But I'm not scared . . . *Am I?*
A ghost is hovering,
and this is bothering
But I'm not scared . . . *Am I?*
The lightning is bright,
and gives us a fright,
But I'm not scared . . . *Am I?*
The shadows sneak,
and we all turn weak,
But I'm not scared . . . *Am I?*
The ghosts, monsters and ghouls,
They're just spooky fools,
But I'm not scared . . . *I certainly am!*

Rachel Durant
King Edward Primary School

WHAT IS BLUE?

The space overhead with the sun and moon,
The azure sea crashing on rocks day after day,
Dolphins splashing in and out of the water.
Blu-tack, sticky on your hands,
Blueberries so juicy they dribble down your chin.

Clare Goodwin (8)
King Edward Primary School

MY OWN SPOOKY POEM

Raging sounds of wind wreak the sky!
The cupboards rattle again and again.
The wind is now shrieking through my ears!
The monster is out there!

Black scary shadows emerge through the trees,
                              looking and staring at me.
Thick black clouds move slowly across the sky
Hard rain starts pouring down on the windows
The monster's out there!

A ray of relief covers my bones as the rain stops . . .
                              then the thunder starts roaring!
I'm all on my own in this old house, terribly scared.
The monster's out there

The cupboards are creaking, thunder is wreaking
                              and now I'm really scared!
When will this storm ever end?
When will this storm ever stop?

Donna Steadman
King Edward Primary School

WHAT IS COLD?

Rain water splashing on me.
Ice lollies, delicious to eat!
Freezers full of snow.
Iceland, a country of ice,
Ski mountains
Cold winds blowing . . .

Scott Randall (8)
King Edward Primary School

SPOOKY!

Windows are clattering!
Teeth are chattering!
Everyone's scared,
But I'm not . . . *am I?*

Lightning flashes!
Thunder crashes!
Everyone's scared,
But I'm not . . . *am I?*

But it's waiting for the ghost
That scares us most!
Everyone's scared,
But I'm not . . .
            Yes I am!

Adam F Ahmed (10)
King Edward Primary School

WHAT IS HOT?

Hot is the lava from the volcano
burning everything inside.
It is the desert that frizzles and fries.
The water in the kettle
boiling and bubbling.
Hot is the fire
Tormenting and deadly.

Liam Wattam (9)
King Edward Primary School

THE STORM - MY POEM

The storm has started, the rain is heavy.
The bright yellow lightning is expanding.
The huge black rain clouds have suddenly burst.

It's so spooky!
Everyone is terrified!
But I'm not . . . am I?

The wind is howling like a ghost on its way to get me.
Thunder exploding with raging anger.
Smashing windows, or is it an alien screaming?

It's so spooky!
Everyone is terrified,
But I'm not . . . *Yes I am!*

Rachel Louise Lee (11)
King Edward Primary School

IN A STORM - MY POEM

The spooky windows are rattling loudly,
The heavy rain is coming down fiercely and quickly,
The rustling wind is whistling loudly,
There might be spooky ghosts trying to frighten and scare us.
My scared friend is trembling rapidly,
Suddenly the horrible storm has stopped raging,
We are not scared as we tiptoe to bed, gladly.

Laura Darley (10)
King Edward Primary School

Spooky - My Poem

Howl goes the wind, patter goes the rain,
chatter go my teeth again and again.

I start to scream! Everyone else does too,
there's something in the corner and . . .
Katie's gone blue!

Howl goes the wind, patter goes the rain,
chatter go my teeth again and again.

Michaela is joking then turns around
and hears a spooky sound.

Howl goes the wind, patter goes the rain,
chatter go my teeth again and again.

Lauren Reddall (11)
King Edward Primary School

What Is Cold?

Fizzy pop
with ice-cubes
As cold as winter.
The North Pole
where Santa Claus lives.
Watery icicles
Dripping in a cave.

Let's suck them!

Hannah Fotheringham (8)
King Edward Primary School

IN A STORM - MY SPOOKY POEM

The storm is coming
With rain running down the window-panes.
With lightning crashing in the sky.
Should I stay or fly away?
. . . I'm not scared, am I?
The wind is swirling left to right,
With doors banging, shaking fiercely
. . . I'm not scared, am I?
I'm feeling alone, sad and weary
Hearing people crying for their mums.
And the children are shivering with fear
Hoping the thunder will stop so that they
Can sleep the stormy night away.

Lisa Goodwin (11)
King Edward Primary School

THE STORM - SPOOKY POEM

The storm is coming,
the rain as well.
I hear thunder.
I see lightning as well,
people are shivering in corners of the room
Oh no! I think I'm frightened too!

I feel frightened, my teeth are chattering
my face has gone blue.
I think I have the flu.
I think I see a monster weeping!
He looks really sad,
but in the end I am glad.

Gemma Holt (10)
King Edward Primary School

WHAT IS HOT?

Food,
  sausages, *frizzly* and *sizzly*.

Volcano,
  Erupting, exploding like a bomb.

Tea,
  hot in a teapot.

Baths,
  Relaxing in a bath.

Radiators,
  in a bedroom, snug and hot.

Charlotte Kyle (8)
King Edward Primary School

BONNIE

I've got a pet called Bonnie.
She's fluffy and scruffy.
She's lovely and cuddly.
I love her.
She's got a soggy nose and
every time she goes for a drink
she wipes it on dad's toes.
She thinks my bum's a cushion,
and she wants to eat our budgie
because he's green.
She's a brave dog.
When dad gets me,
Bonnie saves me.
It would be quiet without her.

Carrie-Ann Mead (7)
Our Lady Of Mount Carmel Primary School

SPRING

Spring is cold and windy
The daffodils are starting to grow.
Daffodils are yellow.
Blossom is coming on the trees.
The bushes and flowers are opening.

Katherine Varga (8)
Our Lady Of Mount Carmel Primary School

HIDE-HOUSE

I have a little hide-house it's up my garden tree.
None of the world can see it, just me.
You have to climb the tree to get there but that doesn't bother me.
You can have a little tea party or you can hide, hide, hide.
That's all you ever do in a hide-house hive.

Amy Anderson (7)
Our Lady Of Mount Carmel Primary School

JEWELS

My mummy had
some jewels and they were red
and she couldn't find them
and she bumped her head.

William Johnson (5)
Our Lady Of Mount Carmel Primary School

EASTER

Easter, Easter!
Here at last,
Now's the time to end my fast.

Eggs galore,
That's the best,
Lots of chocolate to make a mess.

Into town,
With our monies,
We see lots of chicks and Easter bunnies.

Easter Day,
Oh, please come soon,
How many eggs will be in the room?

Mummy's here,
Hip, hip hooray!
Lots of eggs to hunt today.

I feel sick!
Oh dear, oh dear,
Thank goodness Easter comes once a year.

Louise Niles (9)
Our Lady Of Mount Carmel Primary School

TARANTULA

A fast mover
A killer
Cunning catcher
A good alarm
A nest builder
Hairy legs.

Craig Commons (9)
Our Lady Of Mount Carmel Primary School

THE CAT AND THE BAT

I saw a little cat
It was playing up a tree
After a while it spotted a bat
And then opened its eyes with glee!

Little pussy wanted to play
And started to pounce and paw
The bat was eager to get away
But puss caught bat with her claw!

Bat was cross with naughty puss
His wing was tattered and torn
The cat was bored with all the fuss
And cleaned her paws with a yawn!

Bat flew off to tend his sores
Pussy was left to play and bound
The cat lost her grip with her paws
And began to tumble to the ground!

Ffion Jones (6)
Our Lady Of Mount Carmel Primary School

SPRING

When it is spring,
the bluebells sort of ring.
Winter starts resting and,
the birds start nesting.
The children get dirty knees,
and the grown-ups grow green peas.

Kate Stafford (8)
Our Lady Of Mount Carmel Primary School

A FLOWER

Once there was a
flower that grew
on top of a tower.

When it rained
the flower got a
shower.
A boy who
was mad he
saw the flower
he pushed
it over.

I like the
flower.
It is nice
but one day
it died.

Kimberley Gibson (7)
Our Lady Of Mount Carmel Primary School

SEAL

A fish eater
A good swimmer
A clever clogs
A friendly friend
A silly thing
A funny rascal
A lover ball.

Gemma Hizzett (8)
Our Lady Of Mount Carmel Primary School

THE POT DOLL

In the morning I wake up to see
My little pot doll looking at me,
Her eyes are brown
And she wears a crown
That shines very brightly.

She dances round and round,
She is like a dancing clown,
Her hair is long and brown
Which reaches to the ground
That shines very brightly.

When she stops
She falls and flops
My little pot doll
Has gone to sleep
But she still shines very brightly.

Rochelle Muirhead (9)
Our Lady Of Mount Carmel Primary School

MY RABBIT

A warm cuddler
A floppy hopper
A happy sniffer
A lettuce eater
A sunbather
A furry friend
Sensitive ears.

Isabel Gibson (9)
Our Lady Of Mount Carmel Primary School

MY GRANDAD'S HAIRY LEGS

My grandad has such hairy legs
He looks like a big gorilla
My grandma said
When she's in bed
They scratch her, tickle her and scrape her.
I think my grandad's legs are like a coat of fur
Or a woolly, itchy blanket
But what he likes best about his legs
Aren't his knees that look like pegs.
But when his hands are itching
He rubs them on his legs
I think my grandad needs to shave
Because the hairs show through his trousers
So *please* this year just for once,
Don't look like a big gorilla!

Sarah Hagan (9)
Our Lady Of Mount Carmel Primary School

SCHOOL DINNERS

Squishy moss and sloppy gloss
a big mud pie with worms in mine,
But the dinner ladies are witches
and how they itch us,
lumpy rice pudding with a chunk of custard,
Ugh, help! A skunk!
Aaaarrrggghhh! There's a worm down my dress!

Emma Beaglehole (8)
Our Lady Of Mount Carmel Primary School

MY BABY SISTER

My baby sister is so bright,
She fills us all with delight.
Even though she's a little mite,
I love her so much I could take a bite.

My baby sister keeps us up all night,
But we don't mind it's all right.
She laughs all day and likes to play,
I love her so much I want to hide her away.

My baby sister loves us all too,
That's why she always gurgles and coos.
She sits on mummy's knee,
And flies round like a bizzy bee,
That's why I love her you see.

Amy Cummins   (8)
Our Lady Of Mount Carmel Primary School

MY PUPPY

I had a puppy
And he was sad.
So I made him a cookie
And he was glad.

I had a cat
And she was sad.
So I made a mat
And she was glad.

Geneva Milnes (7)
Our Lady Of Mount Carmel Primary School

SOON IT WILL BE SPRING

Soon it will be spring
And what wonders it will bring
Baby animals are newly born
Some are big and some are small

Flowers are popping out of the ground
Blossoms are now all around
I hear some buzzing near
That tree, oh dear me, it's a bumble bee!

I see birds in the sky
Swooping low, swooping high
We are looking forward to the spring
For these wonders it will bring.

Laura Jane Sheldrake (10)
Our Lady Of Mount Carmel Primary School

SNOWY

Snowy is a rabbit, her fur is very white,
Snowy got lost and slept in my room that night.
She slept next to my bed, and kept popping out her head.
She runs around free, it doesn't bother me,
I love Snowy!
She loves me too,
Her eyes are very blue.
She sleeps in a box,
And wears white socks.

Leanne Kelly & Sharna Mulholland (7)
Our Lady Of Mount Carmel Primary School

SPACE

If you are going to space
Put in your case
A rose for your toes
With a bottle of rum to fill your tum
If you don't have a race
You'll never come in first place
So don't try to win
When your award's just going in the bin
But if the rocket's made of tin
Then it will go rattle! Rattle! when it hits the bin
I'll zoom through the sky
I'll zoom past the stars
But the driving I won't try.

Maria Law (8)
Our Lady Of Mount Carmel Primary School

THE LITTLE CLOWN

There was a little clown, his name was Charlie Brown.
He could cry to the sky but none knew why.
I like clowns because they are funny,
but Charlie Brown was not funny.
Charlie the clown got a new job,
he was going to be a dancer.
He danced all day, he danced all night,
but still he was sad then he was glad,
when they said he was a good dancer.

Natasha Pavlovskis (7)
Our Lady Of Mount Carmel Primary School

SPRING

When spring comes
all the flowers grow.
Red ones
Yellow ones
and purple ones
as far as we know.
As we feed them
they grow big.
They might die if we dig.
Daffodils are yellow
tulips are purple.
I love spring
when the flowers grow.

Hannah Honeybone (7)
Our Lady Of Mount Carmel Primary School

IN A PET SHOP

Okay gimmi a hamster.
Okay gimmi a frog.
Okay gimmi a guinea-pig.
Okay gimmi a dog.

Now I have my hamster,
And I like my frog,
But best of all
I totally love
My guinea-pig and dog.

Danielle Winkler (9)
Our Lady Of Mount Carmel Primary School

MUSIC

Class three loves singing, it gets them ringing,
half of them play the violin,
half of them play the drums.
When it's assembly, they sing their hearts out
when it's time to sing the hymns.
Most of them like dancing to pop music,
Some of them like tiptoe ballet dancing.
And most of them like the Spice Girls!
And the radio.
Some of them are in the orchestra playing
the trumpets, the recorders and the cello and violin.
And that's your music lesson from Class three today!

Sally McKenzie (8)
Our Lady Of Mount Carmel Primary School

SPRING

Spring is the time
When it gets warmer.
Flowers come out.
And wake up and grow.
It can be sunny
It can be windy
I like spring, do you?
There are yellow colours
and purple colours.
I like spring, do you?

Ciara Woods (8)
Our Lady Of Mount Carmel Primary School

MY BUDGIE

My budgie is called Billy and he is very silly,
He falls off his perch when he is scratching,
and thinks his reflection is his girlfriend.
He hits the mirror with his beak,
and has also learned how to speak.
'Good morning, give us a kiss,' or
'Hello Billy' are his favourite things to say.
He loses his feathers quite a lot and
makes quite a mess with his seed.
He's nine years old and we all
love him very much indeed.

Sarah Baker (7)
Our Lady Of Mount Carmel Primary School

SCHOOL

I don't want to go to school,
just listen to those boring rules.
I hate school, it's just too boring,
I'd rather be like dad, still in bed snoring.
I try to write with my left hand,
I try to learn but don't understand.
I watch those children go and play,
while all we do is work all day.
I can't wait until school ends
so I can go out and play with my friends.

Kennedy McLaughlin (7)
Our Lady Of Mount Carmel Primary School

BONFIRE

There's a big beast in my garden
shouting, screaming, burning.
He has sharp spiky hair with a bed of ash.
He sits on his bed until he burns out
and all that's left is the bed of ash.
The flames sparking up above the little tree.
Like a display of fireworks.
The red and yellow sparks look like
the beast is rising from its bed of the burnt ash.
The flames crack, crackle beneath the tree.

Greg Male (9)
Our Lady Of Mount Carmel Primary School

INSTRUCTIONS FOR GIANTS

Please do not step on the climbing frame.
Or drink up the swimming pools.
Try not to tread on the teachers.
But please flatten all the schools.

Please do not block out the sunshine.
But duck your head when jets fly by.
Please push all the rain clouds away.
Please mind where you're putting your great big feet.
Please do not step on that *chair!*

Rebecca Jaram (7)
Our Lady Of Mount Carmel Primary School

ICEBERG DEAD AHEAD

Captain there's an iceberg,
An iceberg dead ahead.

Captain to the starboard,
Or else we'll all be dead.

Captain she's hit,
What should we do to save the ship?

Mr Andrews, get Mr Andrews,
It's a mathematical certainty the ship will sink.

Get everyone to put their life-jackets on,
Tell them not to worry.

The third class must wait,
We cannot over crowd.

The third class must jump,
There aren't enough lifeboats.

The Titanic is now dead,
Nobody can save it.

Captain there's an iceberg,
An iceberg dead ahead.

Captain to the starboard,
Or else we'll all be dead.

Rachel Carruthers (11)
Rosedale Primary School

NEVER TRUST ROOM KEEPERS

I was going to Skegness
Everything was fine.
I was going to stay in a spooky hotel
In room number forty-nine.

I saw my room keeper Bernard Stoakes
I couldn't see his head.
Then he turned green and slimy
Into an alien instead.

I opened the door
With my keys on a ball.
Into the dining room
Into the hall.

There were aliens all around me
After the ghastly chase.
Then I got a bonk on the head
Woke up in outer space.

So I've got one thing to warn you
What it doesn't say in my letter.
I saw another boy last night
And things didn't get any better.

Ashley Naylor (9)
Rosedale Primary School

SOUTH WEST

The grass twitches,
the wind fiercely blows,
trees churn,
bright lights are blinding,
I wait excitedly for flowers to bloom.

Ella Pettman (11)
Rosedale Primary School

THE BUTTERFLY SEASON

Butterflies flying in the sky hoping that they would not die.
In the winter when they fly they get blown about.
In the dark night sky by the stars, by the moon,
with a glowing twinkle in the blackness of the sky.
I hope the butterflies do not die as they fly.

Emma Jane Hutchinson (10)
Rosedale Primary School

THE CRYING

In the village at the stroke of dawn
I heard a roar, deep inside I heard a cry.
With so much pain I had to cry.
It is so sad but you're not alone.
There are other animals who feel your pain.

Christopher Elliott (11)
Rosedale Primary School

GATEWAY TO HEAVEN

I often ask myself this question,
is this the gateway to heaven?

Will I ever be a guiding angel,
am I to be a good example.

Should I carry on being myself,
or should I change my ways?

I sometimes pray and ask whatever's there,
because I know He never lies.

I often ask myself this question,
is this the gateway to heaven?

Lucy Kay Welbourn (10)
Rosedale Primary School

SOUTH WEST

Stiff, giants jolting constantly,
the golden sun dazzles.
The sound of boughs crashing,
against a rock, jagged cliff.
The viscous wind howling like a dog,
chasing its prey.

Sarah Hibbert (10)
Rosedale Primary School

THE OCEAN

The sea is gentle but can be rough,
the waves sway from side to side.

Animals swim under the surface,
animals swim like gentle giants
other swim like vicious predators,
sneaking, stalking so that nothing can hear.

The fish sense something bad and swim as fast as they can,
then snap, they're gone.
But the sea is gentle but can be rough,
but most of the time it's alive with fish.

Maxine Watson (10)
Rosedale Primary School

SEAGULLS

Seagulls, seagulls everywhere
Up in the air
Around your hair
Seagulls, seagulls get away
Seagulls, seagulls fly away
Seagulls you better run
The farmer's coming with his gun.

Martyn Vickers (10)
Rosedale Primary School

SADNESS

Sadness hurts deep in the heart,
It slithers like a snake, searching for prey,
It grasps onto you and holds you forever,
It fills you with upset and forces you to cry,
Once you are sad, you weep and cry forever,
You can overcome this sadness,
Just try not to cry,
Then you will not cry,
Now you are happy because you have overcome your sadness,
You will stay happy forever.

Gary Wright (11)
Rosedale Primary School

AUTUMN POEM

Autumn is coming
And the trees are all dying
For the long, cold winter
The trees are all bare
The leaves have fallen down to the ground
The leaves have all crunched
The leaves get very crispy
The leaves change colours
Some turn brown and yellow
And orange
And all kinds of autumn colours
All the plants die
And the sun is gone
The cloud is like a breath of smoke
Waiting to grab you on a windy day.

Gemma Louise Sayer (10)
Sandringham Primary School

THE INN

It was nice and bright,
In the middle of the afternoon.
The mighty inn stood calm and still.
It was made of bricks.
Outside there were flowers as beautiful as can be.
There was ivy hanging down the wall.
It had a place for people to rest and sleep.

James Procter (11)
Sandringham Primary School

FIELDS

The trees are bare.
The hay bales are still.
The sheep are eating in greeny-brown fields.
The colourful sky, shades of pink and purple.
This is a calm day on the farm.
The trees are as still as stone.

Stacey Morgan (10)
Sandringham Primary School

FIREWORKS

Catherine wheels are like hedgehogs.
Sparklers are like midnight stars.
Rockets are like shooting stars.
Cracklers are like snap, crackle and pop.
Roman candles are like flowers and eggs.
Snaky fireworks are like snakes.

Dean Bower (10)
Sandringham Primary School

WHERE AM I?

It's cold and bright,
But there isn't much warmth.
The icicles sparkle in the sun,
I'm surrounded by trees with snow on the top.
There are no leaves around,
The waterfall is frozen,
With icicles stuck to rotten wood.
The waterfall runs down by the side,
Of a big heap of snow and shining ice.

It's like a white blanket,
That's got dirty brown marks on it.
The waterfall once did come down,
Crashing and rushing down a slope,
There was a thunder clap,
Or a booming sound
But now it has all iced up
We won't hear that beautiful sound.

Daniel Hewitt (11)
Sandringham Primary School

A SPECIAL FRIEND

I've got a very special friend,
The one I always knew,
He made me happy and sad sometimes,
He watched my back,
He is a very special friend,
I knew him from nursery,
He's still my friend,
A very good friend and is like a bodyguard.

Daniel Parkin (10)
Sandringham Primary School

CAN'T BE LATE

I am a leaf on a tree,
My green coat has gone instead it's orangey.
All of the leaves have lost their green,
Apart from the leaves which are evergreen.
Shall I jump from my branch,
And fall upon the ground,
Like all the other leaves around?
I think I'll just wait,
I don't mind if I'm late,
But all the others will.
It won't be long before the bell will be rung,
And Christmas carols will be sung!
I'll just have to jump, haven't time to wait,
I just can't afford to be late.

Libby Velta Antons-Jones (9)
Sandringham Primary School

WINTER SCENE

Water rippling calmly,
Sun shining down,
Water changing to red,
Yellow glazing on top.

Snow laying on the grass,
Freezing cold water,
Cold and wet snow,
Twigs standing tall.

Paul Dyer (10)
Sandringham Primary School

ALL BECAUSE I HATE HIM

I'll mangle him, I'll tangle him
I'll grab his neck and strangle him
    All because I hate him

I'll sneak into his room at night
And give him his biggest fright
    All because I hate him

I'll throw him out the top window without even a pillow
And throw his wardrobe out with him and land it right on top of him
    All because I hate him

I'll knock him out, I'll kick his bum
I'll not even feed him a little crumb
    All because I hate him.

Liam Stephenson (9)
Sandringham Primary School

THE VALLEY

The breeze blows the trees side by side
The water peaceful and calm
The sun is shining, the sky reflects in the water
Mountains keep it shady
Trees close together
The valley is wide, a little bunch of trees in the middle
Rocks like cliffs
The sky is blue, the clouds pure white
Trunks like lamp posts, branches like poles so big, so wide.

Peter Meakin (11)
Sandringham Primary School

ONE COLD MORNING

I have numb fingers,
My hands are raw,
The snow is slowly melting,
From the rays of the sun.

This chilly winter morning,
With orange skies,
Old bare trees,
One bitter day.

Aged falling fences,
Huge snow covered fields,
Old broken gates,
And frosty walls.

Mark Allinson (11)
Sandringham Primary School

WORD PICTURE

Water falling, splashing, pouring, sparkling, crashing, clashing.
Then swiftly moving at the bottom, the white water is falling.
The water is falling down the middle of the waterfall.
Lots of trees with bright, green and beautiful leaves.
There are some small rocks on the bank of the water.
There are also some in the water.
There are some little grass shoots shooting/pushing.
The bank is covered with gravel and mud.
Underneath the clear white water there are lots of
broken pieces of rock.

Bree Fox (11)
Sandringham Primary School

FRIENDS

Friends are nice
Friends are sometimes kind
You need friends or you won't survive
Lauren is my nicest friend
But we still fall out all the time
You have to sometimes or another
Friends are helping me
Helpful, that's what I think about friends
You can have small friends or big friends
Some people have different friends
Like imaginary friends
Friends that are faraway and write to each other
But everybody needs a friend.

Rebecca Jane England (9)
Sandringham Primary School

THE DARK AND SHINY NIGHT

I watched the brightness disappear
The darkness begins to unfold
I watched the blazing bonfire burning
Just as I'd been told
The fireworks shot off in the air
My brother complains and says it's unfair
Because he could not shoot off in the sky
Burst into bright colours while escaping the sky
I left that night as happy as ever
I could never forget this night
Never, ever, ever.

Gemma Mulholland (11)
Sandringham Primary School

ANGER

I hate it when my anger,
Just creeps up and strikes,
When I least expect it.

You can see its eyes,
Normally I couldn't
Even hurt a fly.

First I get grounded,
And sent to bed,
Suddenly I think
Why?

Alan Biddleston (11)
Sandringham Primary School

ENEMY

My brother is my worst enemy.
He kicks and punches people and nearly got expelled from school.
He lost his temper.
Slammed the door.
He swears.
He hits me.
He wrecks everything.
He does not like school.
I don't like him.
He is my worst, worst, worst enemy.
I'm sure he is.

Ashley Le Gat (9)
Sandringham Primary School

SPACE

As I travel through the sparkling stars
and colourful planets in my spaceship,
I decide to land and investigate the planet Jupiter.
I hear a strange noise, bzzz.
I walk around and find a strange shaped object.
I try to communicate, 'Hello' I say.
'Bzzz' the object says, 'I am an alien.'

Amy Neidhardt (10)
Shaw Wood Junior School

THE WITCH ON THE BROOM

There sitting is a witch upon a broom,
Casting spells upon a child,
Spelling out frogs, pogs, dogs,
The child begins to spin, twist and turn,
Suddenly changes into *a mouse!*
Black cat smirking.

Jessica Smith (9)
Shaw Wood Junior School

STAR

You are a star,
shining brightly in my heart,
with all you do,
and all you are,
with pride,
and happiness.

Jodie Polson (10)
Shaw Wood Junior School

TODAY IS VERY BORING

Today is very boring,
There's nothing much to do,
There's lions in the laboratory,
And tigers down the loo!

I ask the lions to play with me,
The badgers run away,
I'd like a friend to come to tea,
And play with me all day.

There's an elephant on the landing,
That's just escaped from the zoo!
A mouse is taking him back there,
I wish he'd take me too.

Today is very boring,
I want something to do,
There's no one here to play with me,
Pass me the didgeridoo.

Rachel Doran (10)
Shaw Wood Junior School

THE MISTY PLANET

Looking closely behind the mist a spaceling stood still,
Talking and mumbling to himself,
Standing behind him a dark figure stepped out,
As they stood mumbling to each other,
Something came above them,
They floated up, up and up, soon it vanished,
In the distance were some more spacelings,
As before a spaceship came taking more mumbling spacelings.

Kirsty Tucker (10)
Shaw Wood Junior School

THE BUSY BEE

A black and yellow bee buzzing by,
I start to chase it,
But it flies over the field.
I start to run out of breath,
I start breathing heavy.
There it comes again,
Bzzzz, I wonder why it buzzes?
Why collect honey?
I wish I was a bee.
Why can't we fly?
Just a wonderful animal.
I'm going to try to be a busy bee.
Trip, stumble, ouch, crack.
In hospital.
Nana brings me a present, *a bee.*
Ow no!

Lee Needham (10)
Shaw Wood Junior School

SPACE

Space is dark and lonely
The darkness is all around
Darkness throws a twinkle of light
To you and me, these are stars
The stars make the darkness come alive
Stars brighten the sky
It makes me glad to be alive
Darkness is not as bad as it seems
Twinkling of the stars in the sky.

Jade Harper (10)
Shaw Wood Junior School

THE MONSTER CHASE

Help! The hairy blue monster chasing after me,
Running swiftly I stare forward with icy blue eyes,
The monster is gaining on me,
Opening its mouth showing rotten brown teeth,
Looking at the street name,
Feeling worried,
I am a long way from home,
A dark, spooky alley is up ahead,
It is a shortcut,
Darting down the alley,
The one eyed monster destroys gardens as it flattens trees,
Eventually my house is in sight,
I rush through the door,
The massive monster roars,
I sigh in relief,
At last I am safe.

Matthew Varley (9)
Shaw Wood Junior School

MY DOG

His nose is cold and wet,
His eyes are brown and bright,
He looks after us at night,
He likes big bones and doggy chocs too,
But he never does what he's told to do,
When we go out he lays and waits,
I hear him bark as I shut the gate,
I love him, I do say,
He's my dog, his name is JJ.

Ross Wilson (9)
Shaw Wood Junior School

THE ROCKET

Getting ready to take off,
Ready 5, 4, 3, 2, 1, blast off,
Flying to the moon,
Passing some of the planets,
Taking care of the controls and buttons,
Getting close to the moon,
Landed on the moon,
Wearing big white suits,
Two men having a look round,
Writing notes,
Going back to the earth,
Talking to each other on the rocket,
Discovering things when they got back,
Very happy to be back on earth.

Kerrie Curry (9)
Shaw Wood Junior School

THE SPACE ATTACK

Something shining up in the gloomy space,
A little rocket dazzling in your face,
Something green and shiny too,
Steps out on to Mars,
Mars, Mars think about Mars,
With its tasty centre and
it's lovely chocolate surface,
Oh! Think about Mars,
A little grey alien can cut it in two,
Just for me and you.

Carla Louise Drane (9)
Shaw Wood Junior School

OUTER SPACE

Outer space is far away,
I'd like to go there, some day.
I wonder what it would be like,
Do you think that I could ride my bike?
Gliding through the atmosphere.
I would give a great big cheer - *yippee*

Playing football in the air,
Kicking the ball but not knowing where.
Is there any other life?
I wonder if I'd find a wife?
There's lots of things I'd like to know,
Only one thing for it - I'll have to go.

Michael Varley (10)
Shaw Wood Junior School

THE ROCKET

Once there was a rocket,
A rocket in the sky,
One, two, three then not to be seen,
Maybe it's going to Mars,
Gone past the moon,
There comes fire out the back,
Gone as a flash,
It lands at last,
On the moon,
Then ready to go again,
It flashes its way back to earth.

Amanda Standring (10)
Shaw Wood Junior School

THE TROPICAL ISLAND

Hot sand burning the soles of your feet,
Waves lapping against each other,
Faint footprints disappearing under the small waves,
Small splodges of colour darting about under water,
Under the blue sea,
Yellow, pink and orange corals,
Green seaweed brushing the rocks,
Making them smooth and shiny,
Getting dark,
A gushing waterfall in the distance,
What a cooler shady place to be.

Shorrel Benjamin (10)
Shaw Wood Junior School

THE PIG AND THE BUTCHER

A snout as big as a frying pan,
He lays in the sun and dreams,
Visions of bacon,
Up he gets and runs away,
As fast as he can go,
His face goes redder as he runs as fast as he can,
Crash! He bumps into the butcher,
Which gives him a terrible fright,
The butcher gets angry, really, really angry,
Ties up the pig and gets ready to cook,
Pork chops, bacon, sausages for tea.

Nadine Benjamin (10)
Shaw Wood Junior School

MYSTERIOUS PLANET

A green dot in the velvet sky,
Moves closer and closer,
As I get nearer and nearer,
I land on the still planet,
I shiver,
A chill goes up my spine,
I get out of my rocket,
Something moves behind me,
I turn quickly,
It's a?
Then I wake up and find it's all a dream.

Melissa Steptoe (9)
Shaw Wood Junior School

ON A SUNNY SUNDAY

Come on will you get alive.
It's 12 o'clock and you haven't done anything yet.
Nothing to do!
Why don't you go and play with Mike?
He's gone away for a holiday.
What can I do?
Why don't you go and do some weeding?
Do it yourself.
Well why don't you pick all mum's prize flowers, flood the pond,
throw all the garden gnomes against the garage and smash them.
Pop your sister's brand new football on purpose, dye the grass purple,
paint the window-sills pink, smear mud all over the clean windows,
take the back wheel off your sister's bike so she can't ride it?
I would but I did it an hour ago!

Laura Howard (9)
Walkeringham Primary School

FLOODS

F looding places everywhere
L osing people's lives
O ut of the sky came the rain.
O ozing out of tiny cracks came the water.
D eath is lurking
S o beware.

Jonathan Scott (7)
Walkeringham Primary School

FLOOD

F loods are dangerous.
L ightning flashes.
O ver the fields.
O ver the barns.
D estroying the crops.

Oliver White (6)
Walkeringham Primary School

FLOOD

F loods destroying houses
L ightning flashing
O ver the fields
O ver the farms
D estroying crops.

Nico Vaccari (6)
Walkeringham Primary School

ON A WET AND WINDY WEDNESDAY

What can I do, I am bored?
Why don't you find your brother and play a game with him?
No way, he cheats.
Well why don't you listen to your brand new CD?
Nah.
I know all the songs off by heart and it's getting dead boring
listening to it over and over again.
How about playing with the cat, all she is doing is moping
around getting in my way?
No.
Why not?
Because the last time I played with her the silly thing bit me.
Ermm, why don't you go and wash your hair in the toilet,
take a mud bath, have a mayonnaise shower, eat all of yesterday's
leftovers, cover yourself in mouldy cheese spread and dye your hair
rainbow colours with permanent dye and put orange paint in the
shampoo bottle, put rice pudding in the dishwasher powder,
put ants in your brother's knickers, swap sugar for salt and wipe
bogies down your dad's best shirt?
Nah. I suppose that's boring as well.
No, it's just that I did all that 5 minutes ago.

Louise Barlow (11)
Walkeringham Primary School

PUDDLES

P uddles on the playground
U nderground they run.
D own the drain,
D own, down, down.
L ike a river runs
E ver on to the sea.

Heidi Clinch (6)
Walkeringham Primary School

WHAT I SAID TO THE LIGHTNING

Dear Lightning,
why do you flash?
Why do you strike at night crashing on the ground
Like a canonball falling from sky?
Starting fires.
You blast like fire from a furnace,
You glow in the dark.
You tear away at buildings,
Like a bulldozer.
You strike hard,
Here and there,
Striking the ground-cracking!
You lash out at the trees,
Tearing them apart.
Why do you hurt people?
They haven't hurt you!
Why do you rip tiles off roofs?
You will never have any friends crashing here and there!

Brett Myers (9)
Walkeringham Primary School

THUNDER

T he lightning flashes.
H ere comes a tornado
U p in the sky.
N ow it thunders,
D own comes the rain.
E verything is black.
R ain, rain, wind blows.

Marc Priest (7)
Walkeringham Primary School

SIMPLE SEASONS

S unny
P laces
R abbits
I n
N ice
G ardens

S ummer
U usually
M akes
M ost
E njoy
R esting

A utumn
U mbrellas
T urn
U pside down
M isbehaving
N aughtily

W inter
I s
N ow
T urning
E ven
R ougher.

Kathryn Price (9)
Walkeringham Primary School

TIDAL WAVE

T he water is rough,
I t's swirling around.
D angerous and violent,
A ll destroyed in its power as it
L aunches itself in the air.

W ater rushes through the town
A nd on and on it goes
V ery fast through the gaps.
E ver on till its power runs out.

Matthew Howard (7)
Walkeringham Primary School

SIMPLE SEASONS

S pring   W ith
 P lants   I cey
  R oses   N ights
   I n   T he
    N ice   E arth's
     G ardens   R ock hard

S un   A n
U p   U nusual
M akes   T ime
M e   U ntil
E njoy   M isty
R unning   N ovember.

Sam Bramham (7)
Walkeringham Primary School

TALKING TO THE WEATHER

Dear thunder,

Why are you so loud?
Your blistering sparks of lightning scare people.
Why do you strike at night?
You kill beautiful plants and trees, kids cannot go out and play,
power cuts appear, accidents occur.
The clouds crack like a digger drilling.
You make the ground rattle and you make noises like earthquakes
and buildings get damaged and you will not have any friends,
so please stop scaring people.

Wayne Cockin (11)
Walkeringham Primary School

SIMPLE SEASONS

S pring
P rimroses
R ebloom
I n
N ew
G ardens

A utumn
U sually
T ires
U s
M aking
N oises

S ummer
U sually
M akes
M um
E ats
R ed apples

W inter
I s
N ippy
T o
E veryone
R iding.

Daniel Staples (9)
Walkeringham Primary School

TALKING TO THE WEATHER

What I said to the ice.

Dear ice,
       Why are you so slippery?
       Why are you so bad?
       Why do you hurt us?
       What have we done to you that is so bad?
       Why do you give us bad legs?
       Why do you freeze everything in sight?
       Sometimes the ice is so bad that the cars freeze up.
       Sometimes the people cannot get to work because
       the cars have frozen up.

Sam Lowther (10)
Walkeringham Primary School

FOOD!

I like hot dogs and pizza too.
I like cheese,
And if I want some I always say please.
I like meat,
It's a very tasty treat.
I like sausages,
The way they roll.
I like chips,
I make them do tricks.
I like the jackets that jacket potatoes wear.
If you don't want your food,
I will always be there!

Robert Baxter (8)
Walkeringham Primary School

THAT'S THE SPIRIT

It seems a most rewarding post
Applying as a trainee ghost.
Where one is taught with moans discreet,
To shake and shimmer in a sheet.
A Mr Count Dracula's
He'll pass you as a spook or spectra.
The discipline is strict, it's true,
You speak when you are spoken to,
Until come graduation day,
You've finished everyone away,
A credit to your creepy school.
Well done to every boy and ghoul!

James Hardy (10)
Walkeringham Primary School

A SCHOOL DAY

Wake up!
Wake up!
It's school today.
OK
OK
I pray
I pray.
There's no maths
Or Paul hurling on the grass.
Or tinned potatoes and cheese flan
Oh dear! What a man
Making us all eat *his* cheese flan.
I hate it!
I hate it!
It makes me sick.
If only he wouldn't pick
The egg in the middle.
And after that - games
It's like watching the River Thames -
Then playtime and story.
It's mystery
But it's *boring* history.
But home time comes
I race out to Mum and give her a *big*
Cuddle
Even though she's in a muddle.
Shorts when it's raining
My alarm clock wakes me up
Oh!
It's Sunday!

Hannah Miller (8)
Willow Primary School

KRISTALLNACHT

I heard sounds
I got out of bed
I peeked through the window
There were people fighting
People were dead
I climbed in my own little bed
I heard my windows crash
I heard bangs as well
I went deep, deep down in my bed
And was quiet as a mouse
I heard my mum and dad downstairs
And lots of shouting and yelling
There were people on the landing
I peeked through my bed cover
The door flung open
The light went on
A giant was there
He came and said,
'You are lucky.'
Then went back down the stairs.
In the morning
There was broken glass
Everything was upside-down
Everything except Grandma's vase
I looked outside
Houses were on fire
My mum and dad were crying
Everything was damaged
Even the stairs.

Joanna Henshaw (9)
Willow Primary School

AUTUMN

Conkers, conkers fall to the ground
I collect conkers every autumn day
Even when it's raining
It is fun.
A pocketful of them
Is best.

Elliot Gale (8)
Willow Primary School

AUTUMN

I like autumn with
All the leaves on the ground
And the trees are nearly bare
From the wind the trees are going from side to side
Now the wind blows and blows hard.

Samantha Whiteley (8)
Willow Primary School

A BOY CALLED PAUL

There was a young boy called Paul,
Who learned how to play football,
He went to Old Trafford,
And ended up in Stafford,
And now sells hot dogs on a stall.

Alastair Brown (8)
Willow Primary School

UNDER THE RUBBLE

Under the rubble
It is dark and scary
Under the rubble
I lie and wait
Under the rubble
I think I must be dead
Under the rubble
I hear a dig - dig - digging noise
Under the rubble
A sharp blade comes through
Under the rubble
I crawl free
Out in the world
I see a deserted street
Out in the world
I see a German plane
Out in the world
I see no one
Out in the world
I see nothing.

Richard Hinchliffe (9)
Willow Primary School

THE SKELETON

Today we saw a real skeleton
We only had one half
We had the right half
I was amazed when I held it
It felt smooth and cool
I couldn't believe it was real.

Henry Beevor (8)
Willow Primary School

THE BLITZ BRITS

I hear aeroplanes
Dropping bombs
I have some injuries
Some bruises
And some bumps
I hear fire crackling
Like mad
I think that Germans
Are very bad
I hear
Crying and people dying
I am very worried
About my family and
If they are
Being buried
I am scared
It is very dark
I am in the shelter
In the garden.

Vicki Lacey (8)
Willow Primary School

AUTUMN

Silver grass
In the morning.
The cold wind
On your face
Leaves scattered
All over the place
So scrunchy
Under your feet.

Michael Frosdick (8)
Willow Primary School

The Blitz

I was waiting till
The siren stopped, I heard shouting,
I heard screaming and
Then a *boom!*
It was scary but
My mum said it was next door
Then I heard another
Boom! It hit the top of the house
I was scared so was my mum
Now I have nowhere to live any more
But when I had a look
It was just a tile that had fallen down.
Then I rushed back to the shelter
Then I heard another *boom!*
This one was a real bomb
But it missed the house
And then the siren stopped
I was safe so was my house
I was happy again now.

Paul Richardson (8)
Willow Primary School

Friends

Friends are for playing with,
Friends are for fun,
Friends are for friendship,
Friends are to keep you company,
Friends should like you not hate you,
Friends can help you,
Friends are kind not horrible,
But the best of all is to have plenty of friends.

Rebecca A Sykes (9)
Willow Primary School

THE BLITZ

The noise of the Blitz
Is really scary
You hear shouting and screaming
The noise of bombs and an explosion
Engines, here, there and everywhere
The houses are falling
Smoke everywhere and fire everywhere too.
The sound of bombs and guns
Oh no It's just landed, what a bang
The houses are wrecked and so is mine
The smells are terrible
People are rushing everywhere
Water splashing to put fires out
The sirens are going off
People are dying
It is very scary
Hitler's brought his troops again
The aeroplanes are coming down
I don't know if my family has died!

Thomas White (9)
Willow Primary School

THE CHURCH

There is a bell and it goes ding, dong,
Then there are footsteps in the hall.
Doors bang and make a very loud noise,
Then a heartbeat bangs.
There is a phantom chasing people.
There is a man playing an organ.
There is a piano playing in a church.
There is a drum playing when the phantom's chasing.

Nyssa Blake (9)
Willow Primary School

BRITAIN IN THE BLITZ

I was in bed one night.
I heard the air raid siren.
I rushed down the stairs,
My mum shouted, 'Get in the shelter.'
I was scared,
I looked out of the door,
I saw a bomber,
It dropped a bomb on our house.
My best friend had died.
It was really smoky,
A fire engine came out.
A pipe burst in a fireman's face, I laughed.
Rubble was everywhere,
Another five bombs came over,
I almost choked because of the smoke,
I was wondering if a bomb would hit.
Our house looked like a hill made of rubble.
There were about ten bombers in the sky.
It smelled smoky.

Matthew Payne (9)
Willow Primary School

EARLY MORNING NOISES

Mum yawning,
Dad snoring,
Toilet flushing,
Bag banging,
Floorboards creaking,
Alarm clock ringing,
Doors creaking
And the sun singing.

Scott Chattin (8)
Willow Primary School

HORSES

Horses, horses
That's all I want.
Horses, horses
That's all I need.

The different colours on their fur
The different sizes too.

Horses, horses
That's all I want.
Horses, horses
That's all I need.

The way they jump
Seven foot high is *super!*

Horses, horses
That's all I want.
Horses, horses
I love them.

Rachel Haigh (9)
Willow Primary School

THE SPIRIT

Church bells swinging
Drum beating
Dungeon door shutting
Trees swaying
Keyboards banging
Boots clinking
Heart beating
Spirits flying.

Oliver Churchill (9)
Willow Primary School

THE BLITZ

The sirens went off, not again please,
I got out of bed and ran downstairs,
There was my mum getting the baby
'Come on, quick, Claire, quick.'
The horrid Blitz.
We ran to the shelter, my feet freezing cold,
Hearing the noise of people screaming and shouting,
I could hear the noise of the aeroplanes in the sky,
My baby sister was crying her head off.
The horrid Blitz.
We got in our shelter just in time.
I sat down then all of a sudden a noise went *bang!*
I was so scared, lots of thoughts were going round in my head.
I heard a bomb drop, then another.
I heard people screaming, crying and shouting for help.
I heard a trickle of water
And the crackling of the fire.
The horrid Blitz!

Claire Wragg (9)
Willow Primary School

HAUNTED CHURCH

In a church there were people,
Outside the church were graves.
But one grave had the phantom's name on.
Then suddenly, there came the ghost of the phantom,
The door of the church slammed shut.
The organ has woken the phantom.
He said, 'You woke me up from one thousand years of sleep.'
Then he said, 'You shall pay. You shall pay!'

Michael Peterson (9)
Willow Primary School

THE NIGHT OF DESTRUCTION

Boom!
Hey what was that?
I better go and look out of my window.
Oh no! Hitler is invading
There are a load of fires all over the place
Boom!
That was next door
It will be us next
I can hear screaming, shouting and crying.
Boom!
Help it's hit the roof
It's caved in on me
I wonder what's happened to the rest
The alarm's gone off but I can't get up
I'm stuck under the bricks
Mum and Dad have got out
Hooray, I'm out
I'm going to the shelter now.

Christopher Buckley (9)
Willow Primary School

UNDER THE RUBBLE

Under the rubble there's a great big puddle.
I was under the rubble. I had cuts on my leg.
There was a big explosion and I had a broken leg.
I was crying and there was a big *bang!*
I could hear a siren and there was lots of smoke.
I coughed and coughed.
I felt so sad. I heard lots of cries.
I cried for help but nobody came for me.

Laura Wilbourn (8)
Willow Primary School

CREEPING IN THE BUSHES

Creeping in the bushes is
A small, scuttling mouse.

That is creeping in the bushes.

Creeping in the bushes is
A flash of black and orange.

That is creeping in the bushes.

Creeping in the bushes is
A tiger with a human.

That is creeping in the bushes.

That human was my friend,
Roar!
I gave the warning too late.

So, a tiger was creeping in the bushes.

Hannah Shekle (9)
Willow Primary School

AN AUTUMN POEM

Lovely crusty leaves, falling everywhere,
All the leaves are following everywhere I go.
Children playing with the leaves throwing them around them.
People standing on leaves making them crunch.
The weather is cold.
Like the sea making a noise as it comes forward and back again.
The sun comes out from behind the clouds and shines on the houses.
The grass is wet after all the fog.

Sharlene Duhre (8)
Willow Primary School

THE BLITZ!

Screaming, shouting, crying and dying
They're the things that you would hear
It's so scary and so smoky
It smells bad and I don't like it
Gas mask, bombs and injuries
You hear people shouting
Put out that fire!

That's the Blitz!

I don't like the Blitz at all
I was worried and scared a lot
I wondered if I would live
There were bombs and aeroplanes
Fires, engines, explosions
They are the things that happened
In the blitz.

Kim Norman (8)
Willow Primary School

FOOTBALL!

I am mad about football,
It is a goal scoring game.
People play it all over the world.
That's including girls (but I think they're rubbish)
For World Cup '98, I wanted England to win.
Glory, glory Man United, they are the best team.
That's why they're gonna win the league.
I am mad about football,
It is a goal scoring game.

William Coleman (8)
Willow Primary School

THE AUTUMN SEASON

In autumn things
Happen slowly
Like lovely soft
Leaves change to
Lovely crunchy leaves.

The little squirrel
Hibernates with
Little crunchy nuts
The hedgehog gets
Very fat
Ready for winter.

The birds all fly away
Ready for the winter
And the frost lies on the roof.
I like autumn.

Tiffany Hankinson (7)
Willow Primary School

SPOOKY MUSIC

In a church a phantom rings the bells, then chases everyone.
I run in a room,
My heart is beating very fast,
Then the doors slam
I can't get out.
The phantom gets in and I run out
Then some music starts playing,
And wakes up the other phantoms
And they are chasing after me.

Jessica Barras (9)
Willow Primary School

ROMANS FROM LONG AGO

Romans from long ago
Liked to watch
Gladiator fights and
Chariot racing
Romans from long ago.

Romans from long ago
Believed in many
Gods and goddesses
Jupiter was king of the gods
Romans from long ago.

Romans from long ago
Did lots of things
Chariot racing and
Believed in many gods
Romans from long ago.

Kathryn McColl (8)
Willow Primary School

AUTUMN

I like conkers falling
To the ground
I like picking
Conkers off the ground
I like playing conkers
With my friends
It is fun
The first person
To crack the other wins.

Emma Warren (8)
Willow Primary School

UNDER THE RUBBLE

Under the rubble
There I was
With scary noises above my head
I shiver, I scream
But I'm all alone
I shiver again trying to spot my bed
There's smoke all around me
Big puffs of it I know
The smashing of the windows
I can hear it all
What's happening to me?
And where's my mum?
I try to get out by digging my way there
I fit through the hole just about
I go round and look for my mum
But I won't find her without a doubt.

Melissa Oxley (8)
Willow Primary School

NO MAN'S LAND

There was a church and
There was something there scary
And I was really frightened
Because the door slammed and there was a bang.

I heard a door slam and it frightened me
And I was in horror.
A flute was playing,
My heart was beating fast
And I ran out of the door and screamed loudly.

Samantha Crowther (8)
Willow Primary School

THE BLITZ AT NIGHT

We waited for the sirens
It was about thirty seconds or more
We ran as fast as we could
We reached the shelter, we made it
What do the Germans think they're doing
Who do they think they are?

Suddenly I heard a crash
Like a house falling
I looked up the steps
I saw a German plane falling
From the sky
It seemed as if it hit a building.

I just remembered Digger, my dog
He must be dead. It felt horrible.

Dominic Caunt (9)
Willow Primary School

SKELETON

When I saw the box I knew it was old
When I saw the skull
It was smaller
Than I thought
The bones were very light.
There were more bones than I thought.
At first I was scared
But then I dared to feel
The leg was very smooth
The colour was whitey-brown.

Thomas Falcon (9)
Willow Primary School

UNDER THE RUBBLE

U nderneath my own roof.
N o one to help you
D oodle-bug V1 had hit our house.
E verything on top of me.
R each out from under the rubble.

T he world is destroyed.
H oping it all was a dream.
E verything destroyed.

R each out and pull.
U p you get to see your house destroyed.
B udge everything out of the way.
B ang, bang opening the door.
L ook at your toys broken.
E normous clouds of smoke.

Antony Lunn (9)
Willow Primary School

EARLY MORNING NOISES

Kettle boils
Silver foil
Milk pours
Dad snores
Alarm clock rings
Cockerel sings
People talk
I use my fork
Slipper's tapping
Mummy's napping.

Amadeus Usher (8)
Willow Primary School

An Autumn Poem

Autumn is good
Because we can
See the leaves
All around
The grass
And in autumn
The leaves fall off
The trees
Autumn is good
Autumn is great
Autumn is when
It is getting winter
The trees will rock
And the animals
Will hibernate.

Samantha Shaw (8)
Willow Primary School

Under The Rubble

I was in the bathroom. There was a tremendous noise,
The next I knew, I was under the rubble.
I didn't know what to do.
I tried to put my hand up for help.
I felt air, I was lucky,
I managed to get out.
The first thing I thought about was my family,
I smelled burning, I screamed, I felt scared.
I saw fire and bits of nothing.
I thought I might die.

Racheal Purchase (9)
Willow Primary School

A Frosty Day In Autumn

Here comes Jack Frost
On the snow and ice
Making windows
Frozen as frozen
As ice.
The frost covers
The field and the
Roof tiles look like
Snow and then the
Autumn sun comes up
Jack Frost runs away
The snow and ice is
Melting on an
Autumn day.

Sophia Chambers (8)
Willow Primary School

The Phantom

I am running away from the phantom,
Running past the bells.
Opening a door, banging it shut
Scared stiff am I
My heart is thumping I can hear it loud.
The phantom has got me.
Running away I am
Door banging, it is past
The phantom has gone
The phantom rings the bells once more.

Victoria Ford (9)
Willow Primary School

SPOOKY NOISES

We heard bells ringing and it was spooky,
Then we heard footsteps
And they went on and on until . . .
They stopped and then . . .
Bang
The door slammed shut.
After that we heard a kind of heart beating,
Boom boom, boom boom, boom boom.
The bells kept on ringing.
Then we heard a very loud flute, then . . .
Bang
Then the door slammed shut again
The flute kept on playing.

Emily Wykes (9)
Willow Primary School

RABBITS

Rabbits are grey
Rabbits are fluffy
I like rabbits.

Rabbits are cuddly
Rabbits are jumpy
I like rabbits.

I have got a rabbit
It is called Smokey
I like Smokey.

Kathryn Foster (8)
Willow Primary School

SPRINGTIME

In spring
The flowers
Begin to grow
Like snowdrops
Daffodils and crocuses
And even blossom
Then high in the trees
The birds
Begin to make
Their nests ready
For summertime
It starts to get lighter
And the days get longer.

Carl Tipper (7)
Willow Primary School

EARLY MORNING NOISES

People walking
Mum shouting
Dad snoring
Brother coughing
Toaster on
Kettle on
Postman here
Letterbox clinking
Brother playing
Door banging.

Nadia Akhtar (9)
Willow Primary School

UNDER THE RUBBLE

There was a tremendous noise
As soon as anything, I was under the rubble
I tried to shout for help but no one heard me
I could hear lots of bombs going off
I tried to move my left leg but it was broken
I realised that I was alone
I tried to push all the rubble but it was stuck,
I could hear the siren going off
I made another attempt to push the rubble away,
I could hear a whistle
I felt like I was under ten houses
I felt really scared
I thought I would die.

Sara Horscroft (8)
Willow Primary School

THE BLITZ

I am getting so hot with the fire burning,
The German bombers are above and
I'm not sure when they are going to drop a bomb
To try and kill us.
All that I can hear is, *drip, drop* and screaming.
The sirens are giving me a headache.
The house is nearly falling down and it's on fire.
It really smells horrible and it's making me have a
                              really bad cough.
I wish I was evacuated but I'm not very well
The other friends are having a great time.

Francesca Salt (8)
Willow Primary School

DIFFERENT ANIMALS

Look
Animals to be found
Say they're all around.
Some are fast and some are slow
Some are high and some are low.
Kangaroo, I like to *hop, hop, hop*
Don't ask me why, go ask your pop.
Horse, I like to say *neigh, neigh*
I also like to eat hay.
Cat, I like to say *miaow, miaow*
Dogs like to say *bow wow*
Ah! dog they eat me
Dog, we are different now can you see!

Nicky Hetherington (9)
Willow Primary School

THE BLITZ

The Blitz it's noisy, nasty and smoky,
There's loads of explosions night and day,
It's smelly and scary
There's shouting, crying and screaming.

Its the Blitz

German bombers coming overhead,
It's blackout, switch that light out.
To the shelter everyone before we get bombed,
Climb through the rubble then
We can have a cuddle. We'll huddle together.

Thomas Goodman (9)
Willow Primary School

UNDER THE RUBBLE

Under the rubble,
ABC, 1 2 3,
Dark and scared
What can I see?
Nothing!
Put my hand up
Up I come to the road
Where is my mum?
I shout, 'Mum!'
I can't hear her,
What shall I do?
I am scared
Tears flow down my cheeks.

Jade McDermott (9)
Willow Primary School

AUTUMN

Different coloured leaves,
Falling off the trees,
Scattered on the ground,
Looking to be found,
Frost on the grass,
Shining like brass,
Early in the morning,
A cold frosty morning,
People walking down the street,
Little children eating sweets,
Birds migrating,
Hedgehogs hibernating.

Alice Tucker (8)
Willow Primary School

KNIGHTS

Look there is a knight
He is very, very bright
His armour I can see
Is a bright green
He is going to fight
Oh I wish I was a knight.

The battle is rough
And very tough
Lots of knights get killed
Or get very white
But they can fight
Oh I am glad I am not a knight.

Bethany Smith (8)
Willow Primary School